Golf
LEGENDS

Erin Butler and Jared Siemens

MEDIA ENHANCED BOOKS
AV2
BY WEIGL
ADDED VALUE • AUDIO VISUAL

www.av2books.com

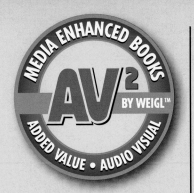

AV² provides enriched content that supplements and complements this book. Weigl's AV² books strive to create inspired learning and engage young minds in a total learning experience.

Your AV² Media Enhanced books come alive with...

Audio
Listen to sections of the book read aloud.

Key Words
Study vocabulary, and complete a matching word activity.

Video
Watch informative video clips.

Quizzes
Test your knowledge.

Go to **www.av2books.com**, and enter this book's unique code.

Embedded Weblinks
Gain additional information for research.

Slide Show
View images and captions, and prepare a presentation.

BOOK CODE

M 4 9 3 6 7 9

Try This!
Complete activities and hands-on experiments.

AV² by Weigl brings you media enhanced books that support active learning.

... and much, much more!

Published by AV² by Weigl
350 5th Avenue, 59th Floor
New York, NY 10118
Website: www.av2books.com

Library of Congress Control Number: 2016956746

ISBN 978-1-4896-5263-8 (hardcover)
ISBN 978-1-4896-5264-5 (softcover)
ISBN 978-1-4896-5265-2 (multi-user eBook)

Printed in the United States of America, in Brainerd, Minnesota
1 2 3 4 5 6 7 8 9 20 19 18 17 16

122016
113016

Project Coordinator: Jared Siemens
Designer: Terry Paulhus

Photo Credits
Every reasonable effort has been made to trace ownership and to obtain permission to reprint copyright material. The publisher would be pleased to have any errors or omissions brought to their attention so that they may be corrected in subsequent printings. The publisher acknowledges Alamy and Getty Images as its primary image suppliers for this title.

Golf
LEGENDS

Contents

AV² Book Code 2

History and Culture 4

The Grand Slam 6

Golf Equipment 8

Greatest Legends 10

Playing the Game 12

Money Makers 14

Golf Courses of the World 16

Coaches and Teachers 18

Grand Slam Winners 20

Quiz 22

Key Words/Index 23

Log on to www.av2books.com 24

History and Culture

Golf is enjoyed all over the world by people of all ages. It is considered a **sophisticated** game that takes skill and practice. Though games similar to golf have been played for centuries, modern golf began in the Netherlands around the fifteenth century. In 1502, golf became popular in Scotland. Its first player was King James IV. In the nineteenth and twentieth centuries, people in England and the United States began to golf and form golfing organizations.

Champion golfer Nick Faldo of Great Britain adjusted his golf swing in the mid-1980s. He then practiced this new swing by hitting 1,500 balls every day for two years. This led to his 1987 British Open win.

Golf has a long tradition in Scotland. The Gleneagles Hotel opened in the 1920s, and is still an iconic luxury hotel and golf destination today.

Etiquette

Etiquette is an important part of golf. The modern version of the sport was played by Scottish royalty. All players and fans follow a strict set of rules on the golf course. The players, for example, are to play the course quickly, so the players behind them are not forced to wait. Players must also be still and quiet while other golfers are playing. Fans watching a game of golf must also be silent during play. Everyone is asked to turn off their cell phones and not post on social media during the game.

The Ryder Cup

Unlike most golf **tournaments**, the Ryder Cup is a team-based competition. It pits 12 players from the United States against 12 players from Europe, and 28 matches are played over 3 days. In the Ryder Cup, the score is not based on the number of **strokes**, like it is in most tournaments. Instead, the score is based on the number of holes each team wins. The Ryder Cup takes place every two years, and it is a fan favorite. In the history of the tournament, the United States holds the record with 25 wins, 13 losses, and 2 ties.

The Green Jacket

The green jacket is awarded to the winner of the Masters Golf Tournament each year. This tradition began in 1937, when members of the Augusta National Golf Club wore jackets to stand out from the crowd and answer questions. Over the years, the green jacket has become an iconic piece of clothing in golf. The Augusta National Golf Club hosts the Masters, and it has official green jackets in several sizes. The Masters winner is awarded a jacket in his size, which he must return after one year. A replica jacket is given to the player to keep.

The Grand Slam

Jimmy Walker, of the United States, played 187 professional tournaments without a win. Then, in 2014, he won three events. In 2016, Walker won the PGA Championship, his first major tournament.

There are four professional golf tournaments that are known as the Grand Slam tournaments, or "the majors." They are the Masters, the U.S. Open, the Open Championship or British Open, and the Professional Golfers' Association (PGA) Championship. No single tournament is officially considered more important than the others. To win a Grand Slam, players must win all four majors in the same calendar year. No player has ever accomplished this feat. Only five players have ever won all four majors during their career, called a Career Grand Slam. Only one player, Tiger Woods, has won all four majors in a row, from 2000 to 2001. Fans and players have different favorite tournaments, but the Masters has the highest television ratings.

Each of the four Grand Slam tournaments has its own prize. The U.S. Open offers the U.S. Open Championship Trophy. It is 18 inches (45.7 centimeters) high, and 6 inches (15.2 cm) wide. It is made of sterling silver, and is engraved with a laurel wreath that surrounds four golfers. At the top is a winged figure that represents victory.

"The Squire"

The first player to win a Career Grand Slam was Gene Sarazen. Nicknamed "The Squire," Sarazen became a Career Grand Slam winner in 1935. Before that, he had won the U.S. Open and the British Open in 1932, and the PGA Championship in 1933. The 1935 Masters had only been created two years earlier, and it was Sarazen's first attempt. On the fifteenth hole, Sarazen made an astonishing **double eagle** that put him in a favorable position to win the tournament. A few holes later, he was a Career Grand Slam winner.

GRAND SLAM RECORDS

5 WINNERS	Gene Sarazen, Ben Hogan, Gary Player, Jack Nicklaus, and Tiger Woods are the five golfers who have **won a Career Grand Slam.**
3 CAREER GRAND SLAMS	Jack Nicklaus and Tiger Woods have each **won 3 Career Grand Slams**—more than any other professional golfer in history.
20 STROKES	Jason Day and Henrik Stenson both hold the record for **most strokes under par** in a major tournament.
18 STROKES	Tiger Woods and Jordan Spieth are tied for the **lowest number of strokes** under par overall in a Masters Tournament.
17 Years 5 Months	Young Tom Morris is the **youngest person to win a major**, at the 1868 British Open.

MAJOR TOURNAMENT WINNERS

Jack Nicklaus **18**

Tiger Woods **14**

Walter Hagen **11**

Ben Hogan **9**

Gary Player **9**

Golf Equipment

Having the right kind of **equipment** is essential for success as a golfer. Over the years, golfers and sports equipment engineers have worked to perfect golf equipment. As technology has improved, so has golf equipment, allowing golfers to have more control, precision, and power as they guide the ball toward the hole. The following pieces of golf equipment are essential to the game.

TEE

The golf tee was invented in 1899 by George F. Grant, one of the first African American golfers. The tee allows players to hit the ball above the ground for a better shot. Before this invention, golfers carried buckets of sand from hole to hole. They used the sand to build a mound from which to strike the ball.

Most golf courses include a dress code to play. In most cases, a collared shirt is required. Shorts must reach the knee. Jeans are not usually allowed. Khaki pants are the most common option.

CLUBS

Players may carry up to 14 golf clubs with them. Each club has a different design, which allows a golfer to hit the ball in different ways. Woods are designed to hit the ball long distances. Irons give players more control. Putters are used only on the greens, for short distances.

GOLF BALL

Originally, golf balls were leather pouches filled with feathers. They were painted white so they could be found in the grass. Later, balls were made of a kind of tree sap that was molded and hardened. Golfers noticed that these balls played better if their surface was scratched or pitted. Today, golf balls have a solid rubber core. They are wrapped with rubber threads and covered by a hard outer shell.

SHOES

Special shoes are not required while playing golf. However, many golfers find them useful. Golf shoes have spikes on the bottom that give the shoe a better grip on the ground. Golf shoes had metal spikes until 1997. That year, Davis Love III won the PGA championship while wearing shoes with plastic spikes. Today, most professional golfers wear plastic spikes. Plastic spikes are lighter and more comfortable.

Greatest Legends

Golf has seen some skilled and groundbreaking players over the years. As the sport and equipment have evolved, so have the players. The sport was once very exclusive, only allowing upper-class men to play. Today, men and women from all backgrounds play professional golf. Golf's social **evolution** has only increased the sport's popularity around the world.

Tiger Woods

Tiger Woods began playing professional golf in 1997, when he was 20 years old. He won the Masters that same year. He had been considered a child prodigy, but no one predicted how much he would impact the sport. At age 24, he became the youngest golfer in history to win a Career Grand Slam. Then, from 2000 to 2001, he won all four major tournaments in a row. Even though this does not count as an official Grand Slam, since all four wins did not happen in one calendar year, Woods is the only golfer to achieve this feat. Woods re-energized the golf world at the start of his career. He continues to play golf today.

Annika Sörenstam

Swedish golfer Annika Sörenstam is considered one of the best female golfers of all time. She began playing professionally in 1992. Over the course of her career, Sörenstam won 72 titles in the Ladies Professional Golf Association (LPGA) and 18 international titles. She also won a record eight Player of the Year awards. Sörenstam retired in 2008, at age 38. In addition to being a golfer, she is also a talented tennis player.

Most Holes in One

The chance of a professional golfer making a hole in one is 1 in 2,500. Most professional golfers may never make one in their career. These players hold the top three spots for most holes in one.

Kathy Whitworth
11

Hal Sutton
10

Robert Allenby
9

Most LPGA Tour Wins

The LPGA was founded in 1950. Like the PGA, the LPGA hosts tournaments all over the world every year. These five women golfers are the top all-time winners.

PLAYER	ALL-TIME WINS
Kathy Whitworth	88
Mickey Wright	82
Annika Sörenstam	72
Louise Suggs	61
Patty Berg	60

Most PGA Tour Wins

Every year, the PGA runs a series of tournaments. The courses can change from year to year, and are located all over the world. These five men have earned the most wins on the PGA Tour circuit.

PLAYER	ALL-TIME WINS
Sam Snead	82
Tiger Woods	79
Jack Nicklaus	73
Ben Hogan	64
Arnold Palmer	62

Jack Nicklaus

Jack Nicklaus is one of the best golfers in history. He has won 18 major championships, more than any other golfer. Nicklaus won his sixth Masters at the age of 46. He is known for his powerful drive from the tee, as well as his abilities on the green. In 1969, the first course that Nicklaus helped design opened. In the 1970s he started a business that designs golf courses all over the world.

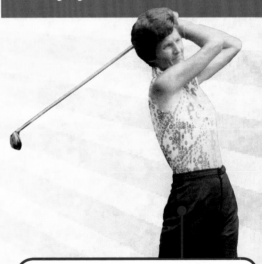

Kathy Whitworth won 88 championships in the LPGA from 1962 to 1985. She was the first female golfer to win more than $1 million in tournament money.

Playing the Game

After his Masters win in 2016, England's Danny Willett was ranked among the world's top 10 golfers for the first time in his career.

Golf follows a strict set of rules. Today, these rules are governed by the Royal and Ancient Golf Club of St. Andrews (R&A) and the United States Golf Association (USGA). The goal of golf is to sink the ball into each of the 18 holes in as few strokes, or swings, as possible. Each hole has a number of strokes a player should try to stay at or under. That number is called par. The player starts in the tee area, where the first stroke is made, and takes a long shot called a drive. Then, the player hits the ball over the **fairway** to the green. The green is a smooth area with a cup sunk into the ground, marked by a pole with flag. The player hits the ball across the green and into the cup. Throughout the game, players try to avoid hazards, such as ponds, trees, and **sand traps**.

One of golf's biggest stars today is Jason Day. He is currently ranked first in the Official World Golf Ranking.

Most Wins After Age 40

Golf is a unique sport in many ways. Unlike most other sports, golfers often continue playing into middle age and beyond. These players had the most wins after turning 40.

PLAYER	WINS
Vijay Singh	22
Sam Snead	17
Kenny Perry	11

Lowest Stroke Total (LPGA)

To win in golf, a player must get the ball into the hole in as few strokes as possible. The number of strokes are tallied to make a player's total score. On the LPGA Tour, these women tied for the lowest score in a 72-hole tournament.

PLAYER	LOWEST SCORE
Karen Stupples	258
Angela Stanford	258
Hee Young Park	258

Youngest to Play in a PGA Tour Tournament

Golfers represent a wide range of ages. Many professional golfers began playing the game when they were very young, and practiced for hours every day. These players were the youngest to play in a PGA Tour tournament.

PLAYER	AGE
Don Dunkelberger *1937 Chicago Open*	11 years, 11 months, 10 days
Michelle Wie *2004 Sony Open*	14 years, 2 months, 29 days
Marshall Springer *1937 Chicago Open*	14 years, 5 months, 11 days

Longest Golf Holes

Golf courses are measured in yards. One of the factors that can make a hole harder to play is its length. These are the longest golf holes in the United States.

841 Yards	**Meadow Farms Golf Course, Hole #12**
800 Yards	**Spring Lake Golf Resort, Hole #6**
777 Yards	**The Links Golf Course, Hole #9**
767 Yards	**Farmstead Golf Links, Hole #18**
747 Yards	**Black Mountain Golf Club, Hole #17** **Turquoise Valley Golf Course, Hole #15**

Michelle Wie was the youngest player to qualify for a United States Golf Association amateur tournament. She began her professional golf career at age 16. She did not win a major tournament until she was 24, at the 2014 U.S. Women's Open.

Money Makers

Golf has become a profitable sport, especially in the second half of the twentieth century. Competitions and tournaments can award huge amounts of money. The average professional golfer makes around $700,000 a year from competitions alone. Golfers also make money by endorsing products for companies. Golf fans contribute to the industry by attending tournaments. An average fan spends nearly $100 at a tournament.

CHEESEBURGER
$6.00

TOURNAMENT FLAG
$30.00

TICKET
(NON-MAJOR TOURNAMENT)
$35.00

HAT
$25.00

TOTAL
$96.00

Largest Tournament Purses

PGA **purses** are split between the winners of each tournament. The golfer who has scored the lowest number of strokes takes home the highest amount of money. Here are the tournaments with the most money offered.

$10.5 MILLION	The Players Championship
$10 MILLION	PGA Championship
$9.7 MILLION	WGC-Cadillac Championship
$9.5 MILLION	WGC-Accenture Match Play Championship
$9.5 MILLION	WGC-Bridgestone Invitational

Sponsor Feature

Automobile manufacturers are the most active golf sponsors in the world. The biggest of these sponsors is BMW. Of all golf courses sponsored by a car company, 27 percent are sponsored by BMW. In total, automotive companies are four times more likely to sponsor a golfer than any other kind of company.

Sporting Salaries

Many professional golfers earn millions of dollars. Some of that money comes from sponsorships, but many also receive large purses, or prize money from winning tournaments. These athletes have earned the most money throughout their careers.

Tiger Woods
$110,061,012

Phil Mickelson
$81,475,338

Vijay Singh
$70,538,688

Jim Furyk
$67,182,502

Ernie Els
$48,757,343

Golf Courses of the World

S omething that players
and fans alike love about
golf is the variety of golf
courses. Each golf course has
its own specific design and
challenges. Everything from
hole length to the number
and kinds of hazards can
vary from course to course.
Most golf courses have 18
holes, which is the number
of holes in a regular round.
These are some of the world's
most interesting golf courses.

Arctic Ocean

Pacific Ocean

NORTH AMERICA

Atlantic Ocean

SOUTH AMERICA

AUGUSTA NATIONAL GOLF COURSE
Augusta, Georgia, United States

Opened for play in 1933, the Augusta National Golf Course has been home to the Masters Tournament since 1934. The Masters is the only major tournament that is played on the same course every year.

ST. ANDREWS OLD COURSE
St. Andrews, United Kingdom

Modern golf developed at St. Andrews Old Course in the 1500s. It is still in use today.

LEGEND
- Land
- Water

N
W E
S

0   2000 miles

3218 kilometers

Arctic Ocean

NULLARBOR LINKS
Ceduna, South Australia
Kalgoorlie, Western Australia

Nullarbor Links is the longest golf course in the world. It stretches across two Australian states, is 850 miles (1,365 kilometers) long, and takes at least three days to complete.

EUROPE

Pacific Ocean

AFRICA

Indian Ocean

AUSTRALIA

DUTCH DOCKLANDS GOLF COURSE
Maldives, Indian Ocean

The world's first floating golf course is currently being built in the Maldives, in the Indian Ocean. With a cost of more than $500 million, it will be the world's most expensive golf course.

Southern Ocean

ANTARCTICA

Coaches and Teachers

Golf coaches act as **mentors** for competitive golfers. Unlike golf teachers, who instruct beginners about the mechanics of golf, coaches help players focus on **strategy** and the big picture of the game. The following coaches have mentored some of the game's greatest players.

Butch Harmon

Butch Harmon is a successful former player who is now a professional golf coach. Harmon has worked with some of the game's best players, including Tiger Woods, Natalie Gulbis, and Phil Mickelson. Known for his quick eye and his ability to see faults that others cannot, he has consistently been voted the top golf instructor in America.

Butch Harmon by the Numbers

1	Book Published *Four Cornerstones of Winning Golf*
$1,000	Hourly Rate for Lessons
5	Signature Academies of the Butch Harmon School of Golf
12	PGA Tour Titles with Phil Mickelson
34	PGA Tour Titles with Tiger Woods

Butch Harmon helped champion golfer Greg Norman change his swing in 1992. This change helped him rise from 53rd place in PGA earnings to number one in the world for that year.

Over the course of his career, Chuck Cook has worked with more than 100 professional golfers, including Payne Stewart and Tom Kite.

Peggy Kirk Bell

Peggy Kirk Bell began as a professional golfer in 1950. She was the founder of the first golf school for women. Kirk Bell was the first woman inducted into the World Golf Teachers Hall of Fame.

Top Golf Coaches

A player's game can change many times over the course of a long career. The right golf coach can help professional golfers win many tournaments. These coaches were voted the best in their field by their peers during the 2015–16 season.

COACH	RANKING
Butch Harmon	1st
Chuck Cook	2nd
Jim McLean	3rd

Most Expensive Golf Coaches

Golf coaches may work with one player for an extended amount of time. They may also work with several players for short periods to help with specific issues in a player's game. These coaches have the world's highest rates.

COACH	RATE
Dave Pelz	$20,000 per day
Hank Haney	$15,000 per day
Ed Hochuli	$3,500 for 3 hours

Originally a research scientist for NASA, Dave Pelz left his job to research golf in the mid-1970s. One of his top students is Phil Mickelson.

Grand Slam Winners

Golf's modern major tournaments include the Masters, the U.S. Open, the British Open, and the PGA Championships. A Grand Slam winner is someone who wins all four of these tournaments in one year. No golfer has ever been able to do this. Five golfers have won all four tournaments during their careers, which is called a Career Grand Slam.

Gene Sarazen

1935 CAREER GRAND SLAM WINNER
NEW YORK CITY, NEW YORK, UNITED STATES

Gene Sarazen began golfing in the 1920s and quickly began to win tournaments. Over the course of his career, he won 39 tournaments, including 7 major championships. He also played on the American team for the Ryder Cup. The year he became a Career Grand Slam winner, Sarazen shot a double eagle from the fairway before winning the Masters title. Sarazen was inducted into the World Golf Hall of Fame in 1974.

Ben Hogan

1953 CAREER GRAND SLAM WINNER
DUBLIN, TEXAS, UNITED STATES

Nicknamed "The Hawk," Ben Hogan was a hardworking perfectionist in golf. He became a professional golfer in 1929 and won three major tournaments before suffering from serious injuries in a car crash in 1949. Doctors thought he would never walk again. However, he not only learned to walk again, he also played golf. He won the British Open on his first attempt in 1953, which gave him a Career Grand Slam.

Gary Player

1965 CAREER GRAND SLAM WINNER
JOHANNESBURG, SOUTH AFRICA

South African Gary Player is the most successful international golfer of all time. He began his professional golf career in 1955 and was the third golfer in history to achieve a Grand Slam with his 1965 win at the U.S. Open. Known for his remarkable fitness and competitive spirit, he won the Australian Open 7 times and the South African Open 13 times.

Jack Nicklaus

1966, 1971, 1978 CAREER GRAND SLAM WINNER
COLUMBUS, OHIO, UNITED STATES

Jack Nicklaus is one of the greatest legends in golf. Nicklaus began golfing at age 10 and turned pro in 1961 at age 21. In 1966, he became a Career Grand Slam winner. That year, Nicklaus made $111,419 in purse money. Today, that would be worth $828,722. He went on to set the record for the most career major championship victories, with 18.

Tiger Woods

2000, 2005, 2008 CAREER GRAND SLAM WINNER
CYPRESS, CALIFORNIA, UNITED STATES

Tiger Woods is one of just two golfers to win three Career Grand Slams. He is a powerful hitter, able to drive the ball more than 300 yards. He is also known for his skillful putting and chipping. Woods was the youngest man as well as the first person of African American or Asian descent to win the Masters.

Quiz

Now that you have read about golf legends, test your knowledge by answering these questions. All of the information can be found in the text. The answers are also provided for reference.

1 In what country did modern golf begin?

A: The Netherlands

2 What piece of clothing does a player win in the Masters?

A: A green jacket

3 What is it called when a player wins the four major golf tournaments in one year?

A: A Grand Slam

4 Which player holds the record for the most wins on the PGA Tour circuit?

A: Sam Snead

5 Which female golfer won 72 titles in the LPGA and was named Player of the Year 8 times?

A: Annika Sörenstam

6 How many holes does a golf course usually have?

A: 18

7 What is the longest golf course in the world?

A: Nullarbor Links

8 Which two players have won three Career Grand Slams?

A: Jack Nicklaus and Tiger Woods

Key Words

double eagle: three strokes under what the officials thought the average number of strokes to be

equipment: items needed for a particular purpose

evolution: the gradual development of something

fairway: the part of the golf course between the tee and the green

mentors: experienced and trusted advisors

purses: amounts of money that are offered as prizes

sand traps: shallow pits filled with sand

sophisticated: having a great deal of worldly experience

strategy: a plan of action

strokes: the act of hitting the ball with a club, and a unit of scoring

tournaments: a series of contests between a number of people trying to win a prize

Index

Bell, Peggy Kirk 19

clubs 9, 13
courses 13, 16, 17, 21

golf balls 4, 8, 9, 12, 13
Grand Slam 6, 7, 10, 20, 22
green jackets 5, 6, 22

Harmon, Butch 18, 19
Hogan, Ben 7, 11, 20

Nicklaus, Jack 7, 11, 21, 22

Palmer, Arnold 11, 15
Player, Gary 7, 21
Professional Golfers' Association (PGA) 6, 11, 13, 15, 18, 22

Royal and Ancient Golf Club of St. Andrews (R&A) 12
Ryder Cup 5, 20

salaries 15
Sarazen, Gene "The Squire" 7, 20
Scotland 4
shoes 9
Snead, Sam 11, 13, 22
Sörenstam, Annika 10, 11, 22
sponsors 15
Stenson, Henrik 7

tees 8, 12

United States Golf Association (USGA) 12

Whitworth, Kathy 11
Wie, Michelle 13
Willett, Danny 7
Woods, Tiger 7, 10, 11, 15, 18, 21, 22

Log on to www.av2books.com

AV² by Weigl brings you media enhanced books that support active learning. Go to www.av2books.com, and enter the special code found on page 2 of this book. You will gain access to enriched and enhanced content that supplements and complements this book. Content includes video, audio, weblinks, quizzes, a slide show, and activities.

AV² Online Navigation

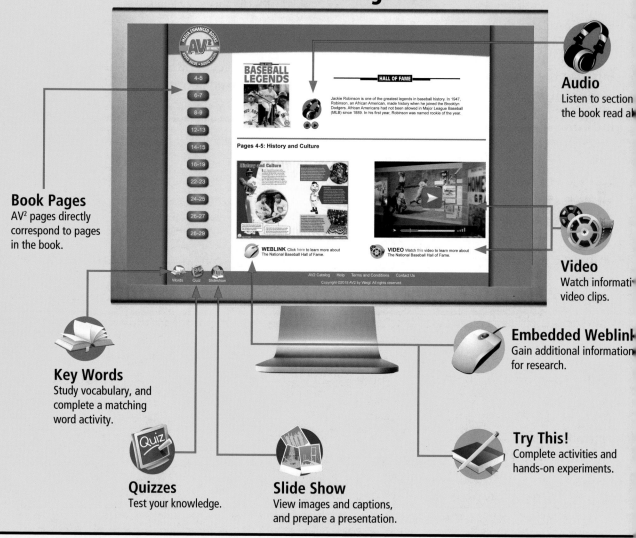

Audio
Listen to section
the book read al

Book Pages
AV² pages directly
correspond to pages
in the book.

Video
Watch informati
video clips.

Embedded Weblink
Gain additional information
for research.

Key Words
Study vocabulary, and
complete a matching
word activity.

Try This!
Complete activities and
hands-on experiments.

Quizzes
Test your knowledge.

Slide Show
View images and captions,
and prepare a presentation.

AV² was built to bridge the gap between print and digital. We encourage you to tell us what you like and what you want to see in the future.

Sign up to be an AV² Ambassador at www.av2books.com/ambassador.

Due to the dynamic nature of the Internet, some of the URLs and activities provided as part of AV² by Weigl may have changed or ceased to exist. AV² by Weigl accepts no responsibility for any such changes. All media enhanced books are regularly monitored to update addresses and sites in a timely manner. Contact AV² by Weigl at 1-866-649-3445 or av2books@weigl.com with any questions, comments, or feedback.